COFFEE: A POEM

Guillaume Massieu
de l'Académie française
Coffee ❧ A POEM

Translated & introduced by
John T. Gilmore

Arc
PUBLICATIONS
2019

Published by Arc Publications
Nanholme Mill, Shaw Wood Road
Todmorden, OL14 6DA, UK
www.arcpublications.co.uk

Design by Tony Ward

978 1910345 79 5 (pbk)
978 1910345 80 1 (hbk)
978 1910345 81 8 (ebk)

Cover design:
Tony Ward

Supported using public funding by
ARTS COUNCIL
ENGLAND
LOTTERY FUNDED

**Arc Publications 'Classics: New Translations of
Great Poets of the Past'
Series Editor: Jean Boase-Beier**

AUTHOR'S ACKNOWLEDGEMENTS

Paul Botley, David Money, Iman Sheeha, Máté Vince and Chantal Wright kindly commented on drafts of the manuscript. For points of information and general encouragement I am particularly indebted to Catherine Bates, Michael Bell, Wanyu Chung, Ingrid De Smet, Thomas Docherty, Letizia Gramaglia, Lynn Guyver, Yasmin Haskell, Eddie Shengchi Hsu, Michael Hulse, Cathia Jenainati, Anthony Ossa-Richardson, Huayan Shao, and Jane Stevenson.

I am especially grateful to the judges of the 2013-2014 John Dryden Translation Competition sponsored by the British Comparative Literature Association and the British Centre for Literary Translation, who commended my verse translation of Massieu's poem. This appeared with a brief prefatory note in *Comparative Critical Studies* 12.1 (2015): 135-142.

My wife Marita and our children, Alex, Annabelle and Giselle, continue to look upon my work with a bemused tolerance for which I am duly thankful.

The usual caveat applies: whatever merit is to be found here owes much to others, but the faults are entirely my own.

CONTENTS

PREFACE

Readers of Wendy Cope's *Making Cocoa for Kingsley Amis* (1986) are probably neither surprised nor disappointed to find that the title poem does not actually say anything about the process of making cocoa. We do not often think nowadays of hot drinks as a subject for poetry, even if cold ones with some alcohol content may still provide inspiration. Cope's readers may well, as she put it in the poem itself, "love the title", but still feel that any detailed exposition of the suggested topic "wouldn't be much of a poem". Better to leave it as it is, just four short lines.

The eighteenth century viewed things rather differently. Yasmin Haskell's work on Jesuit Latin poetry of the period draws our attention to poems on an extraordinary range of topics which the modern reader, still to a significant extent living in the shadow of Romantic notions of poetry being about personal experience and emotion, is likely to consider strange choices – electricity, solar and lunar eclipses, scientific instruments, gardening, and, indeed, hot drinks, with a number of poems being devoted to tea, coffee and chocolate, including a three-book poem on chocolate by the Neapolitan Jesuit Tommaso Strozzi, first published in 1689. One of the most successful of these poems, at least in terms of its number of appearances in anthologies and in translation, was the Abbé Massieu's *Caffaeum, Carmen* (Coffee: A Poem). Nevertheless, my experience of conversations with friends and colleagues suggests that persuading modern readers even to think about reading a poem about coffee originally written in Latin some three hundred years ago is far from easy. The linguistic barrier is a relatively minor problem compared to the changes in taste which have affected generally accepted notions of what constitutes poetry.

With this translation, I seek to introduce modern English-speaking readers to a literary genre which was once enjoyed by educated readers across Europe for several centuries, but which is now likely to seem totally alien – that of didactic poetry in Latin. Massieu's poem is an excellent example: it is relatively short, its subject, coffee-drinking, remains familiar, and the poem can be shown to have been both esteemed by contemporaries and able to attract readers for over a century after its author's death. Above all, it offers a delight in verbal ingenuity and a capacity to entertain, and my translation attempts to convey something of this.

While it is generally accepted that the coffee plant is indigenous to Ethiopia, the origins of coffee drinking remain obscure. It is assumed that the practice originated in Ethiopia, but there is little evidence for coffee consumption elsewhere before the fifteenth century, when it appears to have become popular in the Yemen. The habit spread to Egypt, where it had become common by the early sixteenth century, and from there it passed to Syria and Turkey. As a result of trading contacts, coffee drinking was known in western Europe by the mid-seventeenth century. The visit of a Turkish ambassador to Louis XIV, 1669-70, helped to make coffee drinking fashionable in France, and soon afterwards public coffee houses began to be established. By the end of the seventeenth century it was widespread, and by 1723 there were said to be 380 cafés in Paris alone, with many others in the provinces. By this period, coffee was also popular in other European countries, with the first coffee house in England being one opened in Oxford in 1650, followed by another in London in 1652.

The first work in a European language devoted exclusively to coffee was a short pamphlet published in Latin in 1671 by an author known in Europe by his Latinised name Faustus Naironus or by adaptations of this. He was Merhej ibn Nimrūn (1628-1711), a Maronite Christian whose family came from the village of Bane in northern Lebanon, but who was himself born in Rome and educated at the Maronite College there, later becoming professor of oriental languages at the Sapienza University. Naironus praised the health-giving properties of coffee in extravagant terms, and seems to have been the first writer to print the story of coffee's discovery by the Arab goatherd (or camel-herder) which was taken up by Massieu, and which has been repeated by many later writers. Naironus was soon followed by a proliferation of literary texts of all kinds discussing the social consequences of the habit, and the question of whether coffee was good or bad for you. There were many ephemeral poems and songs about coffee, mostly in vernacular languages, but coffee also featured in the Latin poetry of the period.

Although modern Latin poetry is often neglected in literary histories, the work of Yasmin Haskell, David Money and others has shown how the composition of Latin verse continued to be a lively and successful cultural phenomenon well into the eighteenth century. Thousands of writers saw their Latin verses in print, in book-length anthologies and single-author collections as well as in periodicals, and many more Latin poems circulated in manuscript. Across western Europe, and in European colonial empires in other parts of the world, Latin remained at the heart of any education considered worthy of the name, and the practice of Latin verse composition, that is, learning how to write Latin verse in classical meters in the style of ancient Roman poets, was central to the study of Latin. It was an education with a strong gender bias, but while most (though not all) women were excluded from it, the production and consumption of modern Latin verse was one of the distinguishing characteristics of those who regarded themselves as educated gentlemen, and were so regarded by others. The schools and colleges of the Society of Jesus played a prominent part in education throughout Catholic Europe, and in France, as elsewhere, Jesuits placed considerable emphasis on Latin verse composition in their educational practice. One result was that many of the best known Latin poets of the seventeenth and eighteenth centuries were either priests of the Society of Jesus or taught by them. Among this number was Guillaume Massieu, who was born in the Normandy town of Caen in 1665, of relatively humble origins. His father was a *droguiste*, that is, a hardware storekeeper. After his early schooling in Caen, Massieu was sent at the age of sixteen to Paris, to the Jesuit college which was to be known from 1682 as the Collège de Louis-le-Grand. A promising pupil, he was encouraged to join the Jesuits, and after his noviciate, was sent to teach the humanities at the Collège de Rennes. He returned to Paris to study theology, which he did with success, but the Jesuits' efforts to turn him into a professor of the subject were a failure, as he was unable to summon up for it the enthusiasm which he had for literature, and he left the order in 1695. He was fortunate to find influential patrons, and became a member of the Académie royale des Inscriptions et Médailles (the present day Académie des Inscriptions et Belles-Lettres), and, in 1710, Professor of Greek at the Collège royal de France, followed by his election in 1714 as a member of the Académie française. His last years were clouded by illness, which he suffered with pious resignation, and which did not stop him attending sessions of the two Academies. He died in 1722 at the age of 57.

The date of Massieu's *Caffaeum, Carmen* is uncertain. A stimulus to its composition may have been the appearance of another Latin poem on the same subject, the *Faba Arabica* of Thomas-Bernard Fellon, SJ (1672-1759), which was first published in Lyon in 1696, and to which Massieu's poem shows some resemblance. Alternatively, Massieu's poem may have been begun earlier, dating at least in part from the period when he was teaching humanities and would have been expected to write Latin poems himself as part of the process of teaching his pupils the art of verse composition. We do know it was read at the Académie des Inscriptions, where it was well received, with a contemporary suggesting that, if coffee had been known to Horace and Virgil, it might well have been taken for a classical composition. It may have enjoyed some circulation in manuscript in Massieu's lifetime, but does not seem to have appeared in print until a number of years after his death, when it was published in an anthology in 1738. It appeared in a number of other anthologies and in translations into French and Italian up to the mid-nineteenth century, and a translation in English prose was included in an early twentieth-century work on coffee (see Bibliographical Note). This, which is apparently the only previous English translation, includes a number of errors and, while it is fairly literal, it is also flat, and fails to do justice to the liveliness of Massieu's poem.

It is clear that Massieu's contemporaries regarded him as a model of Latinity. Modern Latin verse was a self-consciously artificial genre in which, as with much eighteenth-century poetry in vernacular languages, the way in which something is expressed, and the manner in which this demonstrates the ingenuity of the writer, is of at least as much importance as the actual content. Massieu treats what might at first seem unpromising topics for poetry as starting points for an elaborate literary game, using similes and periphrasis to create aesthetically pleasing variations on a theme. For example, while his work is a didactic poem in the sense that it tells us about the origins and the real or alleged properties of coffee, and it is in fact possible to prepare a cup by doing what he says, something like the basic instruction to put ground coffee in some water in a pan and then boil it, is drawn out by Massieu to ten lines of verse – seventy-nine words in all. The medium is at least as important as the message, if not more so. Massieu plays the game in an accomplished manner, and consistently maintains a certain lightness of touch and sense of humour conspicuously absent from the work of some contemporary Neo-Latin poets, such as Fellon, or the poems which Pierre Petit (1617-1687) and Pierre-Daniel Huet (1630-1721) devoted to tea.

In translating Massieu's poem, I wanted to keep a sense of both the fact that eighteenth-century Latin verse was a deliberately artificial medium which was very much of its period, and of the way in which verbal ingenuity is treated as an end in itself. As a result, I have used rhyming couplets in imitation of how the poem might have been translated into English by a near contemporary. Although the English heroic couplet is of course very different from the unrhymed quantitative Latin verse which Massieu employed in imitation of classical models, it was widely used in the eighteenth century by translators of both classical and modern Latin poetry. One would not necessarily adopt the same strategy in a modern translation of a classical Latin author, but I felt it was appropriate in this case. While I plan to publish an annotated edition of Massieu's Latin text elsewhere, I hope that this translation can be enjoyed on its own.

John T. Gilmore

Caffaeum, Carmen
Coffee: A Poem

CAFFAEUM, CARMEN

Ut primum in nostras Caffaeum venerit oras,
Divini laticis quae sit natura, quis usus,
Quam praesens homini contra genus omne malorum
Auxilium ferat, hinc facili describere versu
Incipiam. Vos o blandi, vos saepe liquoris
Vim dulcem experti, si nunquam vestra fefellit
Vota, nec eventu spes vestras lusit inani,
Este boni, et nostris facilem date cantibus aurem.

Tuque adeo, cui vim herbarum plantasque salubres
Nosse datum, et tristes membris depellere morbos,
Adsis, Phoebe, favens: nam te quoque muneris hujus
Auctorem esse ferunt: populis tua pandere dona,
Et totum late liceat vulgare per orbem.

Trans Libyam longe, et tumidi septem ostia Nili,
Qua se Asia immensis aperit laetissima campis;
Dives opum variarum, et odoris consita sylvis
Pandit se regio; veteres coluere Sabaei.
Credo equidem, natura, parens illa optima rerum,

COFFEE: A POEM

How *Coffee* first unto our shores was brought,
The many cures this juice divine hath wrought,
Its nature potent 'gainst all human woes,
My song shall now in easy verse disclose.
O ye who've oft its gentle force receiv'd,
If it your wishes ne'er hath once deceiv'd,
Or sportive led your hopes to some ill end,
Then list'ning ears unto our verses lend.

And Thou, to whom is giv'n the healing art
Of plant and herb, who causest to depart
From suff'ring human limbs diseases fell,
Thou, *Phœbus*, aid; for this also they tell
To be Thy gift. Oh, may Thy gifts be found
In ev'ry land, diffus'd the wide world round!

From *Nilus'* seven mouths, from *Libyan* sands
Far off, there once did dwell *Sabæan* bands,
Where happiest *Asia* opes in many a field
Of wealth untold, and woods sweet odours yield.

Hanc sedem ante alias tenero dilexit amore.
Hic semper caeli spirat clementior aura;
Mite soli ingenium; hic alieno tempore flores,
Et foetus varios gravido parit ubere tellus,
Cinnamaque, et casiam, myrramque, et olentia thura.
Illas inter opes, et ruris dona beati,
Ad solem medium conversa, austrosque tepentes,
Sponte sua superas arbor se tollit in auras,
Nusquam alibi veniens, priscisque incognita seclis.
Illa quidem mole haud ingens, non brachia longe
Diffundit patula, aut caelo caput ardua tollit.
Verum humilis, myrti in morem lentaeque genistae,
Surgit humo: dites curvat nux plurima ramos,
Parva, fabae similis, pallenti fusca colore,
Quam tenuis medio distinguit cortice rima.
Hanc adeo nostros plantam traducere in agros
Multi tentarunt, atque omni educere cura,
Nequicquam: neque enim studio votisque serentum
Respondit seges, et longum frustrata laborem
Ante diem in tenera radix exaruit herba:
Seu caeli hoc factum vitio, sive invida tellus
Sufficere apta neget peregrinae pabula plantae.
Quare age, Caffaei quisquis capieris amore,

I that place believe our general mother,
Nature, better loves than any other.
More gentle here the breath of heaven blows,
So that e'en out of season blooms the rose.
The burgeoning earth's with various fruits replete,
Cinnamon, cassia, myrrh and incense sweet.
Among the gifts that bless the country there,
Turn'd to the midmost sun and south winds fair,
A tree grows wild, by human hands not sown,
Not found elsewhere, to ancient times unknown.
Its limbs it spreads not wide, nor yet on high
Its head doth raise unto the lofty sky.
Like myrtle or the pliant broom in kind,
Low it grows; on its branches rich we find
Full many a pale brown berry like a bean,
Upon whose bark a slender cleft is seen.
Many have tried in our own fields to grow
This plant, on it did ev'ry care bestow –
In vain: for to the sowers' wish and pains
The crop ne'er answer'd. Gone their hope of gains:
Despite their toil it withers at the root;
This clime apt food denies the foreign shoot.
O thou who art by *Coffee*'s love possest,

Ne te, Arabum longe summoto ex orbe, salubrem
Accersisse fabam pigeat: namque illius alma
Haec patria est: blandus primum e regionibus illis
Per gentes reliquas fluxit liquor; inde per omnem
Europam atque Asiam, et totum diffunditur orbem.

Ergo quod satis esse tuos cognoris in usus,
Tu longe ante para: largam sit cura quotannis
Collegisse penum, et parva horrea providus imple.
Ut quondam, multo ante memor prudensque futuri,
Colligit e campis segetes, tectisque reponit
Agricola, et curas venientem extendit in annum.
Nec minus interea reliqua est curanda supellex:
Vascula sorbendo non desint apta liquori,
Ollaque, cui collum angustum, sub tegmine parvo,
Cui sensim oblongum venter turgescat in orbem.
Cum provisa tibi haec fuerint: sit proxima cura
Et torrere fabas flammis, et frangere tostas.
Nec cesset multo contundere malleus ictu,
Donec duritiem ponant, penitusque subactae
Exiguus fiant pulvis: quem protinus abde
Aut sacco, aut tales fabricata pixide in usus,
Et corio involve, ac molli circum illine cera,

Grieve not it comes from *Araby* the *Blest*:
The healthful bean there finds its own abode,
Whose merry juice thence to the nations flow'd,
Thence through all *Europe* and through *Asia* too,
So now is *Coffee* found the whole world through.

As much thou know'st as will thy needs demand
Prepare: each year collect with gen'rous hand
An ample store, some little barn to fill.
Last harvest, so the farmer, prudent still,
Did gather from his fields the ripen'd ear
And stor'd his crop against the coming year.
No less meanwhile behoves it thee with care
To fill thy house with other needful gear.
Let there lack not some vessels small design'd
To hold as it is drunk the liquor kind,
Nor pot with narrow neck and little lid,
And belly round in which it may be hid.
With these to hand, the task thou next shalt find,
Will be the beans to roast, and then to grind.
Let not the pestle cease to pound its blows,
Till from the roasted beans their hardness goes,
And work'd on they become the finest dust,

Ne pateant rimae angustae, occultique meatus;
Quos nisi praecludas, furtivo tramite sensim
Particulae tenues, et quicquid purius extat,
Totaque vis vacuas abeat dilapsa per auras.
Est etiam parvae in speciem cava machina turris,
Quam dixere molam; tostae qua munera frugis
Atterere, et crebro possis contundere frictu.
Nucleus in medio, facili versatilis axe,
Aenea contorquet stridente volumina buxo.
Scilicet axis apex capulo transfixus eburno,
Qui manibus versandus erit, per mille recursus,
Mille per et gyros nucleum ciet. Huc ubi glandem
Injicies, capulumque manu currente rotabis,
Haud mora, sub multo raptim crepitantia morsu
Pulveris in morem minui mirabere grana.
Quae contusa semel gremio capit hospite cella
Inferior, capsae fundo interiore reposta.

At quorsum haec autem circum leviora moramur?
Nos majora vocant. Jam dulcem haurire liquorem
Tempus erat, seu cum primi sub lumina solis
Mane novo poscit jejunus pabula venter;
Splendida seu lautae cum post convivia mensae

The which obtain'd, 'tis then with care thou must
Ensure that straightway in a bag 'tis laid,
Or in some box for suchlike purpose made.
Wrap this in hide, and seal with waxen coat
Lest some small crack should gape, through which may float
The tiny specks and what more pure they bear,
And all its strength be lost in empty air.
There is a hollow engine known to fame,
Shap'd like a tower small, a mill by name.
The bounty of the roasted bean is made
A powder thus, with rapid friction bray'd:
The midmost parts on easy axle turn
The grating brass within the boxwood urn;
The axle in an iv'ry handle ends,
Which this way mov'd, then that, the motion sends
To drive the works a thousand circles through.
The handle move as if thy hand it flew
And marvel how the rattling beans straightway
Are lessen'd into dust without delay,
Which in the lower chamber now is stor'd,
Within the coffer deep, a welcome hoard.

But wherefore do these trifles us detain?

Oppressus nimia stomachus sub mole laborat,
Externique impar petit adjumenta caloris.
Ergo age, supposito cum jam olla rubescit in igne,
Jamque tumescentem commixto pulvere lympham
Cernes circum oras fervescere, subtrahe flammis.
Ni facias, subito exundans erumpat aquae vis,
Et laticem inclusum subjectos spargat in ignes.
Quare, ne similis tua turbet gaudia casus,
Sedulus observes, cum jam se non capit unda,
Exultatque aestu: dein ollam terque quaterque
Redde foco, medio dum pulvis in igne vaporet,
Atque superfusae penitus se immisceat undae.
Arte coqui debet blandus liquor, arte bibendus,
Non quo more solent alios haurire liquores.
Namque ubi fumantem rapido subtraxeris igni,
Et sensim fundo faex tota resederit imo,
Non illum impatiens uno libaveris haustu:
Sed potius sorbe paulatim, interque bibendum
Dulces necte moras, et longis tractibus hauri
Exsugens; dum fervet adhuc, uritque palatum.
Tunc etenim melior, tunc intima permeat ossa,
Et sese penitus praecordia in ima, medullasque
Insinuans, vegeto membra irrigat omnia succo.

A greater task demands a loftier strain.
Now is the time to quaff the liquor sweet,
Or if beneath the early Sun's first heat
Our fasting bellies nourishment demand,
Or if the splendours of a dainty board
The stomach burden with too great a load,
Which seeks from outward heat a helping hand.
Come then, the pot upon the fire is fix'd,
The swelling lymph is with the powder mix'd:
As soon thou see'st it at the brim to boil,
Then lift it from the flames or lose thy toil.
Let not the liquor's strength burst forth in haste,
And douse the fire below and go to waste.
Wherefore, lest such a fate thy joys defeat,
Watch till the water bubbles with the heat
No more: then to the hearth the pot restore
To boil again for three times and for four
Until the powder, midmost in the fire,
With all its strength the swelling wave inspire.
With art this liquor should be cooked and drunk,
Not as some other liquors may be sunk:
When thou hast brought it smoaking from the flame,
And to the bottom settled are the lees,

Saepe etiam e fundo quae sursum purior aura
Exiliit, totis illam excepere trahentes
Naribus; in dulci tanta est nidore voluptas.

Jamque hic restabat nostri pars altera coepti,
Divini occultas laticis recludere vires.
Eximias sed quis speret comprendere dotes,
Et tam magna sequi miracula posse canendo?
Namque ubi secreto penetravit in ilia lapsu,
Intus agens sese, vitalem in membra calorem
Inspirat, laetumque afflat sub pectore robur.
Tum si quid crudi est, admixto concoquit igne,
Occultasque vias paulatim, et tenuia laxat
Spiramenta, quibus se trudat inutilis humor,
Et totis fugiant morborum semina venis.

Quare agite, o! vestrae vobis si cura salutis,
Vos queis propendet triplex in pectora mentum,
Qui tardum magno trahitis molimine ventrem,
Vos decet imprimis calido indulgere liquori.
Namque malam humorum, quae vestros obruit artus,
Colluviem coquit, et sudoris corpore toto
Proliciet rivos: nec longum tempus, obesi

Let not impatience with one draught it claim,
But slow, with little sips to take will please,
Not all at once, but drink with sweet delays,
While yet 'tis warm, and on thy palate plays.
So better to thy very bones 'twill flow,
Deep within thy bosom and thy marrow,
Through ev'ry limb the liv'ning juice will go.
Oft from the very bottom of the cup
A purer air, which drinkers will sniff up
With nostrils wide, doth rise – the liquor's spent,
But still there's great delight in such sweet scent.

To show remains part of this task of ours,
What hath this juice divine of secret powers –
Who can hope the knowledge of such gifts t'attain,
Or yet in song their wonders great t'explain?
For downwards when its hidden course it takes,
And deep within its presence felt it makes,
Through ev'ry limb it sends a vital heat
And 'neath the heart a joyful strength doth seat,
With fire added, digests whate'er is raw,
Each secret passage opes and slender pore

Paulatim tumor incipiet decrescere ventris,
Oppressosque artus injusta mole levabit.
Felices populi, quos primo lumine Titan
Aspicit exoriens! Hic Bacchi largior usus
Non unquam nocuit: laticem libare Lyaeum
Lex et sacra vetant: Caffaeo hic vivitur: ergo
Hic laetis agitant florentes viribus aevum,
Et quid sint morbi, ignorant, quid filia Bacchi
Lautitiaeque comes podagra, et quae foedere pacto
Innumerae nostrum pestes grassantur in orbem.

Nec minus et tristes pellit de pectore curas,
Exhilaratque animos almi vis blanda liquoris.
Vidi aliquem, dulci sese cum nectare nondum
Proluerat, lento taciturnum incedere gressu.
Triste supercilium, et tetricis frons aspera rugis.
Idem vix dulci guttur perfuderat haustu,
Haud mora, contractae fugiebant nubila frontis,
Gaudebatque omnes salsis aspergere dictis.
Non tamen hi quenquam risu assectantur amaro,
Nec liquor innocuus laedendi inspirat amorem.
Virus abest, blandique placent sine felle cachinni.
Atque hic in toto mos est Oriente receptus,

Through which the useless humours find their way
From ev'ry vein drives seeds of sickness and decay.
   Come ye, by worries for your health distress'd –
Each with his triple chin upon his breast,
Who each a belly slow to move must strain –
By you in chief this hot draught should be ta'en.
The filthy humours, which your limbs do yet
O'erwhelm, it will dissolve; in streams of sweat
Your body wash; and, by degrees it soon begins,
The swelling of your belly round it thins,
And from your burden'd joints as time shall pass
It lifts the weight, takes off the cruel mass.

   Happy peoples! How happy must they be,
Whom *Titan* rising with's first light doth see!
No harm came ever here from *Bacchus'* use,
Both law and faith forbid *Lyæan* juice:
By *Coffee* here they live, and so enjoy
In strength their span of years, without alloy –
To them, the ills which dainty feasts attend
Unknown, those *Bacchus'* daughter, *Gout*, doth send,
And all the many plagues so near allied
Which half the sick-beds of our world bestride.

Jamque peregrinum tu servas, Gallia, morem,
Potando in vicis Caffaeo publica tecta
Ut pateant. Invitat euntes pensile signum,
Aut hedera, aut laurus. Huc tota ex urbe frequentes
Conveniunt, et grata diem per pocula ducunt.
Cumque semel tepido incaluit mens icta vapore,
Tunc rixae dulces, jucundaque jurgia gliscunt:
Fit strepitus, festo resonat vicinia plausu.
At nunquam epotus mentes liquor obruit aegras.
Quin potius, siquando oculos sopor urget inertes,
Mensque hebet, et torpent obtusae in corpore vires;
Somnum oculis, segnem fugat imo e corde veternum.
Quare his profuerit dulci se aspergere rore,
Queis longi incumbit series immensa laboris,
Quosque opus est studium in seras extendere noctes.

And sad cares *Coffee* chases from our hearts;
Joy to our minds its gentle strength imparts.
One have I seen, who ere the nectar sweet
He'd tasted, silent enter with slow feet,
And look severe, and brow with wrinkles bound.
Yet he, soon as the beverage sweet he'd down'd
And from his knitted brow fled ev'ry cloud,
With witty sayings straightway pleas'd the crowd.
But none are thus to cruel scorn inclin'd,
Or rous'd to hate, who drink this liquor kind:
From malice free their merriment we find.
All through the *East* this custom holds its sway –
A foreign custom *Gaul* doth now obey;
Each street opes doors for *Coffee*-drinking wide,
Hangs signs of laurel or of ivy up,
Which call the city's wanderers inside,
To pass the day with many a pleasing cup.
When once its tepid vapour warms the mind
We gentle brawls and soft contention find,
And all around the hubbub rings with merry jest.
Ne'er by this drink are wayward minds oppress'd,
But when with sleep one's heavy eyes are lull'd,
The sluggish mind, and bod'ly powers dull'd,

Atque hic, quis blandi laticis monstraverit usum,
(Nam virtus latuit multos ignota per annos)
Expediam, et prima repetens ab origine pandam.
Ducebat teneras ad pascua nota capellas
Pastor Arabs: illae errabant per devia tesqua,
Tondebantque herbas; multis cum turgida baccis,
Nusquam visa prius, sese illis obtulit arbor.
Continuo, ut poterant humiles contingere ramos,
Incipiunt crebro frondes convellere morsu,
Et teneros carpunt foetus: invitat amaror.
Nescius interea molli sub gramine pastor
Cantabat, sylvisque suos narrabat amores.
At postquam exoriens campis decedere vesper
Admonuit, saturumque gregem sub tecta reduxit,
Sensit oves molli non claudere lumina somno,
Sed mira praeter solitum dulcedine laetas
Per totam noctem saltu exsultare petulco.

Sleep from the eyes, sloth from the heart, wilt drive.
These then, themselves should wet with this sweet dew
Who must an end to endless tasks contrive,
Or tireless thumb their books the long night through.

   Who first this liquid's uses kind reveal'd
(Whose strength thro' many a year remain'd conceal'd)   }
Is now a truth by me at last unseal'd.
An *Arab* herdsman led his goats to grass,
But they now wand'ring through rough places pass,
And crop herbage there, when with berries swell'd
A tree appears, which they had ne'er beheld.
Straightway, as they could reach the branches low,
They 'gan to seize the green with bites not slow,
And pluck the tender fruit, whose bitter taste allures.
Their herdsman meanwhile knows not what they do,
But fits his tales to rhyme the whole day through:
Out to the woods in song his loves he pours.
At length admonish'd by the evening star,
He homeward drives his flock. Well fed they are,
Yet they close not their eyes in gentle sleep
As they were wont to do in times now past,
But all night caper, each with butting leap.

Obstupuit subita trepidus formidine pastor,
Atque haec fraude mala vicini, et carmine demens
Ac magicis fieri putat artibus. Haud procul inde
Augustas sedes secreta in valle locarat
Sancta manus Fratrum, queis Divum psallere laudes
Cura erat, et meritis onerare altaria donis.
At quanquam magno per noctem rauca tumultu
Obstreperet campana, sacramque vocaret in aedem,
Illos saepe toro properans aurora morantes
Repperit, oblitos media consurgere nocte:
Tantus amor somni. Praeerat sanctae arbiter aedi
Longaevus Senior, moderabaturque volentes,
Canitie multa capitis barbaque verendus.
Hunc pastor festinus adit, remque ordine narrat,
Auxilium implorans.Senior sub pectore risit.
Ire juvat, causamque rei explorare latentem.
Ut ventum in colles, permixtos matribus agnos
Ignoti cernit fruticis corrodere baccas.
Atque, Haec causa mali, exclamat: nec plura locutus,
Extemplo teretes gravida legit arbore foetus,
Fertque domum, tritosque in pura diluit unda
Igne coquens, pateramque ingentem interritus haurit.

With sudden fear the herdsman stands aghast,
Craz'd with the thought some neighbour's wish to harm
By magic arts hath done this, or some charm.
Within a hidden valley close at hand,
Made they their rev'rend seat a holy band
Of *Brothers*, each one vow'd GOD's praise to sing,
And to His altars gifts deservèd bring.
But though at night full loud the bell would sound
And summon all to prayer with brazen cries,
In bed the hast'ning dawn them often found,
Unmindful that they should at midnight rise:
So great their love of sleep. There did preside
O'er the holy house an *Elder* as their guide,
Respected for his hoary head and beard beside.
To him the herdsman speeds and tells his tale of woe;
The *Elder* inward smiles, is pleas'd to go,
The matter's hidden causes to unfold.
As crops may be laid waste by tempests bold,
So now he sees the shrubs unknown gnaw'd bare
By nanny-goats and kids their tender care.
" 'Tis this the cause!" he said; with no word more
He berries round from laden bushes bore,

Continuo calor it venis, diffusa per artus
Vivida vis, pulsusque senili e corpore languor.
Tum demum invento Senior sibi munere laetus
Gratatur, fratresque bonus partitur in omnes.
Olli certatim, primae sub tempora noctis,
Suavibus indulgent epulis, et grandia siccant
Pocula: nec jam illis molli decedere lecto,
Ut prius, et dulcem labor est abrumpere somnum.

O fortunati, quorum praecordia dulcis
Saepe lavit liquor! Haud illorum pectora segnis
Torpor habet: vegeti praescripta ad munia surgunt,
Et primi gaudent praevertere luminis ortum.
Vos quoque, queis cura est divino pascere mentes
Eloquio, dictisque animos terrere nocentum,
Vos etiam blando decet indulgere liquori.
Scilicet invalidum firmat latus; acer in artus
Hinc gliscit vigor, et toto se corpore fundit.
Hinc vestrae veniet nova vis, nova gratia voci.
Vos autem, infesti quos vexant saepe vapores,
Queis aegrum importuna quatit vertigo cerebrum,
Eja agite, in dulci praesens medicina liquore est,
Nec tenues alius melior componere fumos.

Which ground at home, with water boil'd and pains,
He boldly from a mighty goblet drains.
In ev'ry limb the lively heat soon dwells,
And weakness from the old man's flesh expels.
Joyful with what he for himself has found,
He shares it with his brothers all around.
These now, in th'early watches of the night compete
In drinking deep, their pamper'd selves with dainties treat,
For they no longer, as before, do dread
Their sleep to break, and leave the comforts of their bed.
How blest by Fortune they, who often feel
This gentle liquor through their innards steal!
A slothful dullness seizes not their hearts –
They hasten to each task their Rule imparts,
And joy to rise before the dawn's first light.
You too, whose words should guilty souls affright,
Whose eloquence divine must feed the list'ner's mind,
You likewise it behoves to taste this liquor kind.
Indeed all weakness of the voice it cures:
New strength of speech, new grace of discourse yours, }
As quick'ning force through all your limbs it pours. }
And you, by hostile vapours often vex'd,
Whose brains by dizziness are oft perplex'd,

Has ipsi, ut perhibent, vires insevit Apollo:
Res est digna cani. Phoebei montis alumnos
Haec quondam invasit capiti infensissima pestis.
Grassatur late, cerebroque illabitur imo.
Jam tota hoc morbo gens ingeniosa laborat,
Desertaeque suis languent cultoribus artes.
Pars etiam morbum simulat, fictumque dolorem
Praetendens, vitae sese devovit inerti.
Displicet ingratus labor; exitialis ubique
Gliscit mollities; curarum, operumque solutos,
Securae cunctos juvat indulgere quieti.
Non tulit ulterius multum indignatus Apollo
Noxia tam blandae contagia serpere labis.
Utque omnem posthac fingendi vatibus ansam
Eriperet, diti e gremio telluris amicam
Elicuit plantam, qua non praesentior ulla
Seu fessum studiis animum reparare labori,
Sive importunos capitis lenire dolores.

No better physic can with this compare
Those slender fumes t'assuage, or calm all care.
These powers did *Apollo's* self bestow,
They say, a tale worth telling as I'll show.
Parnassus' pupils by a strange disease
Of old did find their heads indiff'rence seize,
Which permeates their frames both far and wide,
And reaches deep within their brains inside.
Now all the witty race this plague constrains,
And none for *Art* will take the slightest pains.
Some unreal aches proclaim, and sickness feign,
That they may to a life of ease attain.
The dangerous softness enters everywhere,
Delighting all who've cast off work and care.
No longer can the God enrag'd endure
The spread of this contagion so impure:
That poets to deceive may have no cause,
From *Earth's* rich lap this friendly plant he draws.
None better is the weary spirit to restore
Of him whose life to study is giv'n o'er,
And so permit him, now refresh'd, once more
His labours to resume. Nor can we find
A better cure for headaches' pains unkind.

O planta, humano generi data munere Divum,
Non tibi plantarum e numero certaverit ulla.
Te propter nostro solvunt e littore nautae,
Ventorumque minas, syrtesque atque horrida saxa
Impavidi exsuperant: almo tu germine vincis
Dictamnum, ambrosiamque, et odoriferam panaceam:
Te tristes fugiunt morbi: tibi semper adhaeret
Fida valetudo comes, et laetisssima turba
Garrulitas, rixaeque leves, dulcesque susurri.

Plant, by whose gift the GODS do man befriend,
No other plant with thee can e'er contend.
For thee do sailors from our shores depart,
And brave both winds and rocks with fearless heart.
With thy kind seed thou canst their claims defeat –
Ambrosia, dittany, and panacea sweet.
While from thy presence all sad humours flee,
A joyful crowd shall ever thee attend –
Light jests, and chatter from all ill-will free,
With whispr'rings soft, and *Health*, most faithful friend.

The Latin text of Massieu's poem is based on that first published in Pierre-Joseph d'Olivet, ed., *Poetarum ex Academia Gallica, Qui Latine, aut Graece scripserunt, Carmina* (Paris: Boudet, 1738), pp. 289-301. Ligatures (such as "quæ" for "quae", and the ampersand) have been expanded. I have followed the practice of most modern editors of Neo-Latin texts in omitting the accents which were commonly used in Latin texts from the Renaissance to the eighteenth century, on the grounds that these are more likely to be a distraction to modern readers than a help to pronunciation or understanding. In two instances (at l. 1 and l. 14) the 1738 text prints the first word of the line in all caps to indicate the beginning of a verse paragraph; this is not done consistently throughout the poem, and I have capitalised only the first letter. The long s (ſ) has been replaced with the ordinary version of the letter throughout. The space between a word and punctuation marks other than a full stop has been omitted. In other respects, spelling, capitalisation, and punctuation follow the 1738 text.

An anonymous Italian translation in blank verse, *Il Caffè, Poema Didascalico*, appeared as part of a bilingual edition (n.p., n.d.; but c. 1740).

An anonymous translation in French prose appeared as "Le Caffé [sic], Poëme," in the *Journal Oeconomique* (Paris, July 1756), pp. 40-52, while a different translation in French prose was published in Anon., *Étrennes à tous les amateurs de café* (Paris, 1790); reissued with an additional preface as *Traité du Café, Contenant l'Histoire, la Déscription, la Culture et les Propriétés de ce Végétal* (Paris, 1798).

Augustin Théry included a translation of the poem in French rhyming couplets in his *Notice sur l'Abbé Massieu* (Caen: A. Hardel, 1854).

A translation in English prose was published in William H. Ukers, *All about Coffee* (2nd ed., New York: The Tea and Coffee Trade Journal Company, 1935; facsimile reprint, Mansfield Centre, Connecticut: Martino Publishing, 2011). Ukers's statement that "The following translation of the poem from the Latin original was made for this work" leaves it uncertain whether he himself was the translator, or it was commissioned from someone else who has not been credited.

Biographical information about Massieu is taken mainly from Théry. The story of the goatherd first appears in Faustus Naironus, *De Saluberrima Potione Cahue seu Café nuncupata Discursus* (Rome: Michael Hercules, 1671), where he is introduced as "a certain keeper of camels, or, as others call him, of goats," though there is no mention of camels in Massieu's poem. Naironus's pamphlet later appeared in an English version, by a translator who signed his dedication with the initials C. B., but is otherwise unidentified, under the title *A Discourse on Coffee: Its Description and Vertues* (London: Geo. James for Abel Roper, 1710). On the history of coffee-drinking in France in the period, and coffee's presence in contemporary literature, see Alfred Franklin, *Le Café, le Thé et le Chocolat* (Paris: Librairie Plon, 1893). On coffee and material culture, see Rose-Marie Herda-Mousseaux, Patrick Rambourg, and Guillaume Séret, *Thé, Café ou Chocolat? Les Boissons exotiques à Paris au XVIIIe Siècle* (Paris: Paris Musées, 2015), the catalogue of an excellent exhibition held at the Musée Cognacq-Jay. On coffee-drinking in England in the period, see Markman Ellis, *The Coffee House: A Cultural History* (London: Weidenfeld and Nicolson, 2004). For modern Latin verse and its cultural importance, see Yasmin Annabel Haskell, *Loyola's Bees: Ideology and Industry in Jesuit Latin Didactic Poetry* (Oxford: Oxford University Press for the British Academy, 2003), and D. K. Money, *The English Horace: Anthony Alsop and the Tradition of British Latin Verse* (Oxford: Oxford University Press, for the British Academy, 1998).

BIOGRAPHICAL NOTES

GUILLAUME MASSIEU was born in Caen in 1665, and although he came from a humble background, he was sent to Paris at the age of sixteen to study with the Jesuits at the Collège de Louis-le-Grand, one of the most prestigious educational institutions in France. There he acquired a love of literature which led him to baulk at the desire of his superiors to turn him into a teacher of theology, and he eventually left the Jesuits in 1695. Supported by influential patrons, he became a member of the Académie royal des Inscriptions et Médailles, and, in 1710, Professor of Greek at the Collège royal de France. In 1714 he was elected a member of the Académie française. Afflicted by money worries and health problems in his last years, including cataracts which left him totally blind for a period until he had one eye operated on, he nevertheless continued his scholarly pursuits until his death in 1722 at the age of 57.

Massieu's extensive writings included translations from ancient Greek and studies of classical and modern literature and culture. In his lifetime, and for long afterwards, however, he was best known as a writer of Latin, and particularly as a writer of Latin verse, and his poem on coffee was published several times, in the original Latin and in various translations, in the century and a half after his death.

JOHN T. GILMORE was educated in Barbados and in England, and worked in Barbados for fourteen years, including four years teaching at the Cave Hill campus of the University of the West Indies. In 1996, he joined the University of Warwick as a lecturer in the Centre for British and Comparative Cultural Studies (later Centre for Translation and Comparative Cultural Studies), before moving in 2009 to the Department of English and Comparative Literary Studies, where he is now a reader. In the past, he has also worked as a civil servant, in an advertising agency, and as a journalist.

His research interests include British and Caribbean literature in the long eighteenth century in English and Latin; the history of translation in the eighteenth century; Orientalism; and issues relating to the reception of classical literature and to Latin, race and gender. He is particularly interested in eighteenth-century Latin verse and its rôle as cultural capital, and in the history of translation into Latin verse as a means of introducing European readers to non-European literatures.

Previous translations include *Musæ Anglicanæ Anglicè Redditæ: A selection of verse written in Latin by British poets of the eighteenth century* (Coventry: The Derek Walcott Press, 2007), and he is the author of the volume on *Satire* in the New Critical Idiom series (London: Routledge, 2017).

www.ingramcontent.com/pod-product-compliance
Lightning Source LLC
LaVergne TN
LVHW041237080426
835508LV00011B/1259